ISM Code

INTERNATIONAL SAFETY MANAGEMENT CODE

and guidelines on
implementation of the
ISM Code

2010 Edition

INTERNATIONAL
MARITIME
ORGANIZATION

London, 2010

Published by the
INTERNATIONAL MARITIME ORGANIZATION
4 Albert Embankment, London SE1 7SR
www.imo.org

Third edition 2010

Printed in the United Kingdom by CPI Books Limited, Reading RG1 8EX

ISBN 978-92-801-5151-0

IMO PUBLICATION
Sales number: IB117E

Copyright © International Maritime Organization 2010

This publication has been prepared from official documents of IMO, and every effort has been made
to eliminate errors and reproduce the original text(s) faithfully. Readers should be aware that,
in case of inconsistency, the official IMO text will prevail.

015638

Contents

Foreword

With the entry into force, on 1 July 1998, of the 1994 amendments to the International Convention for the Safety of Life at Sea (SOLAS), 1974, which introduced a new chapter IX into the Convention, the International Safety Management (ISM) Code was made mandatory. Chapter IX was amended by resolution MSC.99(73), which entered into force on 1 July 2002, and by resolution MSC.194(80), which entered into force on 1 January 2009.

The Code's origins go back to the late 1980s, when there was mounting concern about poor management standards in shipping. Investigations into accidents revealed major errors on the part of management, and in 1987 the IMO Assembly adopted resolution A.596(15), which called upon the Maritime Safety Committee to develop guidelines concerning shipboard and shore-based management to ensure the safe operation of ro–ro passenger ferries.

The ISM Code evolved through the development of the Guidelines on management for the safe operation of ships and for pollution prevention, adopted in 1989 by the IMO Assembly as resolution A.647(16), and the Revised Guidelines, adopted two years later as resolution A.680(17), to its current form, the International Management Code for the Safe Operation of Ships and for Pollution Prevention (International Safety Management (ISM) Code), which was adopted in 1993 as resolution A.741(18). This Code was amended in December 2000 by resolution MSC.104(73), and these amendments entered into force on 1 July 2002. It was further amended in December 2004 by resolution MSC.179(79), and these amendments entered into force on 1 July 2006. It was further amended in May 2005 by resolution MSC.195(80), and these amendments entered into force on 1 January 2009. The ISM Code was also amended in December 2008 by resolution MSC.273(85). This resolution was adopted on 1 January 2010, and the amendments will enter into force on 1 July 2010.

In 1995, the IMO Assembly, recognizing the need for uniform implementation of the ISM Code and that there might be a need for Administrations to enter into agreements in respect of the issuance of certificates by other Administrations in accordance with SOLAS chapter IX and the ISM Code, adopted the Guidelines on implementation of the International Safety

Management (ISM) Code by Administrations by resolution A.788(19). These Guidelines were replaced with Revised Guidelines, which were adopted by resolution A.913(22) in November 2001, which revoked resolution A.788(19). Guidelines on implementation of the International Safety Management (ISM) Code by Administrations were adopted by resolution A.1022(26) in December 2009. This resolution revokes resolution A.913(22) with effect from 1 July 2010.

This publication includes the texts of SOLAS chapter IX, the ISM Code and the Guidelines referred to in the previous paragraphs. Additionally, Guidelines for the operational implementation of the International Safety Management (ISM) Code by Companies, Guidance on the qualifications, training and experience necessary for undertaking the role of the designated person under the provisions of the International Safety Management (ISM) Code and Guidance on near-miss reporting are included.

International Convention for the Safety of Life at Sea, 1974, as amended

Chapter IX – Management for the safe operation of ships

Management for the safe operation of ships

Chapter IX* of the annex to the 1974 SOLAS Convention

Regulation 1
Definitions

For the purpose of this chapter, unless expressly provided otherwise:

1   *International Safety Management (ISM) Code* means the International Management Code for the Safe Operation of Ships and for Pollution Prevention adopted by the Organization by resolution A.741(18), as may be amended by the Organization, provided that such amendments are adopted, brought into force and take effect in accordance with the provisions of article VIII of the present Convention concerning the amendment procedures applicable to the annex other than chapter I.

2   *Company* means the owner of the ship or any other organization or person such as the manager, or the bareboat charterer, who has assumed the responsibility for operation of the ship from the owner of the ship and who on assuming such responsibility has agreed to take over all the duties and responsibilities imposed by the International Safety Management Code.

3   *Oil tanker* means an oil tanker as defined in regulation II-1/2.22.[†]

---

* Chapter IX of the annex to the 1974 SOLAS Convention was adopted by the 1994 SOLAS Conference. It was accepted on 1 January 1998 and entered into force on 1 July 1998. The text was amended by resolution MSC.99(73) in December 2000, and these amendments entered into force on 1 July 2002. It was also amended by resolution MSC.194(80) in May 2005, and these amendments entered into force on 1 January 2009.

† i.e., "the oil tanker defined in regulation 1 of Annex I of the Protocol of 1978 relating to the International Convention for the Prevention of Pollution from Ships, 1973".

4   *Chemical tanker* means a chemical tanker as defined in regulation VII/8.2.*

5   *Gas carrier* means a gas carrier as defined in regulation VII/11.2.†

6   *Bulk carrier* means a ship which is constructed generally with single deck, top-side tanks and hopper side tanks in cargo spaces, and is intended primarily to carry dry cargo in bulk, and includes such types as ore carriers and combination carriers.

7   *Mobile offshore drilling unit (MODU)* means a vessel capable of engaging in drilling operations for the exploration for or exploitation of resources beneath the sea-bed such as liquid or gaseous hydrocarbons, sulphur or salt.

8   *High-speed craft* means a craft as defined in regulation X/1.‡

Regulation 2
Application

1   This chapter applies to ships, regardless of the date of construction, as follows:

> **.1**   passenger ships including passenger high-speed craft, not later than 1 July 1998;
>
> **.2**   oil tankers, chemical tankers, gas carriers, bulk carriers and cargo high-speed craft of 500 gross tonnage and upwards, not later than 1 July 1998; and
>
> **.3**   other cargo ships and mobile offshore drilling units of 500 gross tonnage and upwards, not later than 1 July 2002.

---

* i.e., "a cargo ship constructed or adapted and used for the carriage in bulk of any liquid product listed in chapter 17 of the International Bulk Chemical Code".

† i.e., "a cargo ship constructed or adapted and used for the carriage in bulk of any liquefied gas or other product listed in chapter 19 of the International Gas Carrier Code".

‡ i.e., "a craft capable of a maximum speed, in metres per second (m/s), equal to or exceeding $3.7\nabla^{0.1667}$ where ∇ = volume of displacement corresponding to the design waterline (m^3) excluding craft the hull of which is supported completely clear above the water surface in non-displacement mode by aerodynamic forces generated by ground effect".

2   This chapter does not apply to government-operated ships used for non-commercial purposes.

Regulation 3
Safety management requirements

1   The company and the ship shall comply with the requirements of the International Safety Management Code. For the purpose of this regulation, the requirements of the Code shall be treated as mandatory.

2   The ship shall be operated by a company holding a Document of Compliance referred to in regulation 4.

Regulation 4
Certification

1   A Document of Compliance shall be issued to every company which complies with the requirements of the International Safety Management Code. This document shall be issued by the Administration, by an organization recognized by the Administration, or at the request of the Administration by another Contracting Government.

2   A copy of the Document of Compliance shall be kept on board the ship in order that the master can produce it on request for verification.

3   A Certificate, called a Safety Management Certificate, shall be issued to every ship by the Administration or an organization recognized by the Administration. The Administration or organization recognized by it shall, before issuing the Safety Management Certificate, verify that the company and its shipboard management operate in accordance with the approved safety management system.

Regulation 5
Maintenance of conditions

The safety management system shall be maintained in accordance with the provisions of the International Safety Management Code.

Regulation 6
Verification and control

1   The Administration, another Contracting Government at the request of the Administration or an organization recognized by the Administration shall periodically verify the proper functioning of the ship's safety management system.

2   A ship required to hold a certificate issued pursuant to the provisions of regulation 4.3 shall be subject to control in accordance with the provisions of regulation XI/4. For this purpose such certificate shall be treated as a certificate issued under regulation I/12 or I/13.

International Safety
Management Code

International Safety Management Code

Resolution A.741(18) as amended by
MSC.104(73), MSC.179(79), MSC.195(80)
and MSC.273(85)

PREAMBLE

1   The purpose of this Code is to provide an international standard for the safe management and operation of ships and for pollution prevention.

2   The Assembly adopted resolution A.443(XI), by which it invited all Governments to take the necessary steps to safeguard the shipmaster in the proper discharge of his responsibilities with regard to maritime safety and the protection of the marine environment.

3   The Assembly also adopted resolution A.680(17), by which it further recognized the need for appropriate organization of management to enable it to respond to the need of those on board ships to achieve and maintain high standards of safety and environmental protection.

4   Recognizing that no two shipping companies or shipowners are the same, and that ships operate under a wide range of different conditions, the Code is based on general principles and objectives.

5   The Code is expressed in broad terms so that it can have a widespread application. Clearly, different levels of management, whether shore-based or at sea, will require varying levels of knowledge and awareness of the items outlined.

6   The cornerstone of good safety management is commitment from the top. In matters of safety and pollution prevention it is the commitment, competence, attitudes and motivation of individuals at all levels that determines the end result.

PART A – IMPLEMENTATION

1   GENERAL

1.1   Definitions

The following definitions apply to parts A and B of this Code.

1.1.1   *International Safety Management (ISM) Code* means the International Management Code for the Safe Operation of Ships and for Pollution Prevention as adopted by the Assembly, as may be amended by the Organization.

1.1.2   *Company* means the owner of the ship or any other organization or person such as the manager, or the bareboat charterer, who has assumed the responsibility for operation of the ship from the shipowner and who, on assuming such responsibility, has agreed to take over all duties and responsibility imposed by the Code.

1.1.3   *Administration* means the Government of the State whose flag the ship is entitled to fly.

1.1.4   *Safety management system* means a structured and documented system enabling Company personnel to implement effectively the Company safety and environmental protection policy.

1.1.5   *Document of Compliance* means a document issued to a Company which complies with the requirements of this Code.

1.1.6   *Safety Management Certificate* means a document issued to a ship which signifies that the Company and its shipboard management operate in accordance with the approved safety management system.

1.1.7   *Objective evidence* means quantitative or qualitative information, records or statements of fact pertaining to safety or to the existence and implementation of a safety management system element, which is based on observation, measurement or test and which can be verified.

1.1.8 *Observation* means a statement of fact made during a safety management audit and substantiated by objective evidence.

1.1.9 *Non-conformity* means an observed situation where objective evidence indicates the non-fulfilment of a specified requirement.

1.1.10 *Major non-conformity* means an identifiable deviation that poses a serious threat to the safety of personnel or the ship or a serious risk to the environment that requires immediate corrective action or the lack of effective and systematic implementation of a requirement of this Code.

1.1.11 *Anniversary date* means the day and month of each year that corresponds to the date of expiry of the relevant document or certificate.

1.1.12 *Convention* means the International Convention for the Safety of Life at Sea, 1974, as amended.

1.2 Objectives

1.2.1 The objectives of the Code are to ensure safety at sea, prevention of human injury or loss of life, and avoidance of damage to the environment, in particular to the marine environment and to property.

1.2.2 Safety management objectives of the Company should, *inter alia:*

.1 provide for safe practices in ship operation and a safe working environment;

.2 assess all identified risks to its ships, personnel and the environment and establish appropriate safeguards; and

.3 continuously improve safety management skills of personnel ashore and aboard ships, including preparing for emergencies related both to safety and environmental protection.

1.2.3 The safety management system should ensure:

.1 compliance with mandatory rules and regulations; and

.2 that applicable codes, guidelines and standards recommended by the Organization, Administrations, classification societies and maritime industry organizations are taken into account.

1.3 Application

The requirements of this Code may be applied to all ships.

1.4 Functional requirements for a safety management system

Every Company should develop, implement and maintain a safety management system which includes the following functional requirements:

.1 a safety and environmental-protection policy;

.2 instructions and procedures to ensure safe operation of ships and protection of the environment in compliance with relevant international and flag State legislation;

.3 defined levels of authority and lines of communication between, and amongst, shore and shipboard personnel;

.4 procedures for reporting accidents and non-conformities with the provisions of this Code;

.5 procedures to prepare for and respond to emergency situations; and

.6 procedures for internal audits and management reviews.

2 SAFETY AND ENVIRONMENTAL-PROTECTION POLICY

2.1 The Company should establish a safety and environmental-protection policy which describes how the objectives given in paragraph 1.2 will be achieved.

2.2 The Company should ensure that the policy is implemented and maintained at all levels of the organization, both ship-based and shore-based.

3 COMPANY RESPONSIBILITIES AND AUTHORITY

3.1 If the entity who is responsible for the operation of the ship is other than the owner, the owner must report the full name and details of such entity to the Administration.

3.2 The Company should define and document the responsibility, authority and interrelation of all personnel who manage, perform and verify work relating to and affecting safety and pollution prevention.

3.3 The Company is responsible for ensuring that adequate resources and shore-based support are provided to enable the designated person or persons to carry out their functions.

4 DESIGNATED PERSON(S)

To ensure the safe operation of each ship and to provide a link between the Company and those on board, every Company, as appropriate, should designate a person or persons ashore having direct access to the highest level of management. The responsibility and authority of the designated person or persons should include monitoring the safety and pollution-prevention aspects of the operation of each ship and ensuring that adequate resources and shore-based support are applied, as required.

5 MASTER'S RESPONSIBILITY AND AUTHORITY

5.1 The Company should clearly define and document the master's responsibility with regard to:

.1 implementing the safety and environmental-protection policy of the Company;

.2 motivating the crew in the observation of that policy;

.3 issuing appropriate orders and instructions in a clear and simple manner;

.4 verifying that specified requirements are observed; and

.5 periodically reviewing the safety management system and reporting its deficiencies to the shore-based management.

5.2 The Company should ensure that the safety management system operating on board the ship contains a clear statement emphasizing the master's authority. The Company should establish in the safety management system that the master has the overriding authority and the responsibility to make decisions with respect to safety and pollution prevention and to request the Company's assistance as may be necessary.

6   RESOURCES AND PERSONNEL

6.1   The Company should ensure that the master is:

.1   properly qualified for command;

.2   fully conversant with the Company's safety management system; and

.3   given the necessary support so that the master's duties can be safely performed.

6.2   The Company should ensure that each ship is manned with qualified, certificated and medically fit seafarers in accordance with national and international requirements.

6.3   The Company should establish procedures to ensure that new personnel and personnel transferred to new assignments related to safety and protection of the environment are given proper familiarization with their duties. Instructions which are essential to be provided prior to sailing should be identified, documented and given.

6.4   The Company should ensure that all personnel involved in the Company's safety management system have an adequate understanding of relevant rules, regulations, codes and guidelines.

6.5   The Company should establish and maintain procedures for identifying any training which may be required in support of the safety management system and ensure that such training is provided for all personnel concerned.

6.6   The Company should establish procedures by which the ship's personnel receive relevant information on the safety management system in a working language or languages understood by them.

6.7 The Company should ensure that the ship's personnel are able to communicate effectively in the execution of their duties related to the safety management system.

7 SHIPBOARD OPERATIONS

The Company should establish procedures, plans and instructions, including checklists as appropriate, for key shipboard operations concerning the safety of the personnel, ship and protection of the environment. The various tasks should be defined and assigned to qualified personnel.

8 EMERGENCY PREPAREDNESS

8.1 The Company should identify potential emergency shipboard situations, and establish procedures to respond to them.

8.2 The Company should establish programmes for drills and exercises to prepare for emergency actions.

8.3 The safety management system should provide for measures ensuring that the Company's organization can respond at any time to hazards, accidents and emergency situations involving its ships.

9 REPORTS AND ANALYSIS OF NON-CONFORMITIES, ACCIDENTS AND HAZARDOUS OCCURRENCES

9.1 The safety management system should include procedures ensuring that non-conformities, accidents and hazardous situations are reported to the Company, investigated and analysed with the objective of improving safety and pollution prevention.

9.2 The Company should establish procedures for the implementation of corrective action, including measures intended to prevent recurrence.

10 MAINTENANCE OF THE SHIP AND EQUIPMENT

10.1 The Company should establish procedures to ensure that the ship is maintained in conformity with the provisions of the relevant rules and regulations and with any additional requirements which may be established by the Company.

10.2 In meeting these requirements, the Company should ensure that:

.1 inspections are held at appropriate intervals;

.2 any non-conformity is reported, with its possible cause, if known;

.3 appropriate corrective action is taken; and

.4 records of these activities are maintained.

10.3 The Company should identify equipment and technical systems the sudden operational failure of which may result in hazardous situations. The safety management system should provide for specific measures aimed at promoting the reliability of such equipment or systems. These measures should include the regular testing of stand-by arrangements and equipment or technical systems that are not in continuous use.

10.4 The inspections mentioned in 10.2 as well as the measures referred to in 10.3 should be integrated into the ship's operational maintenance routine.

11 DOCUMENTATION

11.1 The Company should establish and maintain procedures to control all documents and data which are relevant to the safety management system.

11.2 The Company should ensure that:

.1 valid documents are available at all relevant locations;

.2 changes to documents are reviewed and approved by authorized personnel; and

.3 obsolete documents are promptly removed.

11.3 The documents used to describe and implement the safety management system may be referred to as the Safety Management Manual. Documentation should be kept in a form that the Company considers most effective. Each ship should carry on board all documentation relevant to that ship.

12 COMPANY VERIFICATION, REVIEW AND EVALUATION

12.1 The Company should carry out internal safety audits on board and ashore at intervals not exceeding twelve months to verify whether safety and pollution-prevention activities comply with the safety management system. In exceptional circumstances, this interval may be exceeded by not more than three months.

12.2 The Company should periodically evaluate the effectiveness of the safety management system in accordance with procedures established by the Company.

12.3 The audits and possible corrective actions should be carried out in accordance with documented procedures.

12.4 Personnel carrying out audits should be independent of the areas being audited unless this is impracticable due to the size and the nature of the Company.

12.5 The results of the audits and reviews should be brought to the attention of all personnel having responsibility in the area involved.

12.6 The management personnel responsible for the area involved should take timely corrective action on deficiencies found.

PART B – CERTIFICATION AND VERIFICATION

13   CERTIFICATION AND PERIODICAL VERIFICATION

13.1   The ship should be operated by a Company which has been issued with a Document of Compliance or with an Interim Document of Compliance in accordance with paragraph 14.1, relevant to that ship.

13.2   The Document of Compliance should be issued by the Administration, by an organization recognized by the Administration or, at the request of the Administration, by another Contracting Government to the Convention to any Company complying with the requirements of this Code for a period specified by the Administration which should not exceed five years. Such a document should be accepted as evidence that the Company is capable of complying with the requirements of this Code.

13.3   The Document of Compliance is only valid for the ship types explicitly indicated in the document. Such indication should be based on the types of ships on which the initial verification was based. Other ship types should only be added after verification of the Company's capability to comply with the requirements of this Code applicable to such ship types. In this context, ship types are those referred to in regulation IX/1 of the Convention.

13.4   The validity of a Document of Compliance should be subject to annual verification by the Administration or by an organization recognized by the Administration or, at the request of the Administration, by another Contracting Government within three months before or after the anniversary date.

13.5   The Document of Compliance should be withdrawn by the Administration or, at its request, by the Contracting Government which issued the Document when the annual verification required in paragraph 13.4 is not requested or if there is evidence of major non-conformities with this Code.

13.5.1 All associated Safety Management Certificates and/or Interim Safety Management Certificates should also be withdrawn if the Document of Compliance is withdrawn.

13.6 A copy of the Document of Compliance should be placed on board in order that the master of the ship, if so requested, may produce it for verification by the Administration or by an organization recognized by the Administration or for the purposes of the control referred to in regulation IX/6.2 of the Convention. The copy of the Document is not required to be authenticated or certified.

13.7 The Safety Management Certificate should be issued to a ship for a period which should not exceed five years by the Administration or an organization recognized by the Administration or, at the request of the Administration, by another Contracting Government. The Safety Management Certificate should be issued after verifying that the Company and its shipboard management operate in accordance with the approved safety management system. Such a Certificate should be accepted as evidence that the ship is complying with the requirements of this Code.

13.8 The validity of the Safety Management Certificate should be subject to at least one intermediate verification by the Administration or an organization recognized by the Administration or, at the request of the Administration, by another Contracting Government. If only one intermediate verification is to be carried out and the period of validity of the Safety Management Certificate is five years, it should take place between the second and third anniversary dates of the Safety Management Certificate.

13.9 In addition to the requirements of paragraph 13.5.1, the Safety Management Certificate should be withdrawn by the Administration or, at the request of the Administration, by the Contracting Government which has issued it when the intermediate verification required in paragraph 13.8 is not requested or if there is evidence of major non-conformity with this Code.

13.10 Notwithstanding the requirements of paragraphs 13.2 and 13.7, when the renewal verification is completed within three months before the expiry date of the existing Document of Compliance or Safety Management Certificate, the new Document of Compliance or the new Safety Management Certificate should be valid from the date of completion of the renewal verification for a period not exceeding five years from the date of expiry of the existing Document of Compliance or Safety Management Certificate.

13.11 When the renewal verification is completed more than three months before the expiry date of the existing Document of Compliance or Safety Management Certificate, the new Document of Compliance or the new Safety Management Certificate should be valid from the date of completion of the renewal verification for a period not exceeding five years from the date of completion of the renewal verification.

13.12 When the renewal verification is completed after the expiry date of the existing Safety Management Certificate, the new Safety Management Certificate should be valid from the date of completion of the renewal verification to a date not exceeding five years from the date of expiry of the existing Safety Management Certificate.

13.13 If a renewal verification has been completed and a new Safety Management Certificate cannot be issued or placed on board the ship before the expiry date of the existing certificate, the Administration or organization recognized by the Administration may endorse the existing certificate and such a certificate should be accepted as valid for a further period which should not exceed five months from the expiry date.

13.14 If a ship at the time when a Safety Management Certificate expires is not in a port in which it is to be verified, the Administration may extend the period of validity of the Safety Management Certificate, but this extension should be granted only for the purpose of allowing the ship to complete its voyage to the port in which it is to be verified, and then only in cases where it appears proper and reasonable to do so. No Safety Management Certificate should be extended for a period of longer than three months, and the ship to which an extension is granted should not, on its arrival in the port in which it is to be verified, be entitled by virtue of such extension to leave that port without having a new Safety Management Certificate. When the renewal verification is completed, the new Safety Management Certificate should be valid to a date not exceeding five years from the expiry date of the existing Safety Management Certificate before the extension was granted.

14 INTERIM CERTIFICATION

14.1 An Interim Document of Compliance may be issued to facilitate initial implementation of this Code when:

> .1 a Company is newly established; or

> .2 new ship types are to be added to an existing Document of Compliance,

following verification that the Company has a safety management system that meets the objectives of paragraph 1.2.3 of this Code, provided the Company demonstrates plans to implement a safety management system meeting the full requirements of this Code within the period of validity of the Interim Document of Compliance. Such an Interim Document of Compliance should be issued for a period not exceeding 12 months by the Administration or by an organization recognized by the Administration or, at the request of the Administration, by another Contracting Government. A copy of the Interim Document of Compliance should be placed on board in order that the master of the ship, if so requested, may produce it for verification by the Administration or by an organization recognized by the Administration or for the purposes of the control referred to in regulation IX/6.2 of the Convention. The copy of the Document is not required to be authenticated or certified.

14.2 An Interim Safety Management Certificate may be issued:

 .1 to new ships on delivery;

 .2 when a Company takes on responsibility for the operation of a ship which is new to the Company; or

 .3 when a ship changes flag.

Such an Interim Safety Management Certificate should be issued for a period not exceeding 6 months by the Administration or an organization recognized by the Administration or, at the request of the Administration, by another Contracting Government.

14.3 An Administration or, at the request of the Administration, another Contracting Government may, in special cases, extend the validity of an Interim Safety Management Certificate for a further period which should not exceed 6 months from the date of expiry.

14.4 An Interim Safety Management Certificate may be issued following verification that:

 .1 the Document of Compliance, or the Interim Document of Compliance, is relevant to the ship concerned;

 .2 the safety management system provided by the Company for the ship concerned includes key elements of this Code and has been assessed during the audit for issuance of the

Document of Compliance or demonstrated for issuance of the Interim Document of Compliance;

.3 the Company has planned the internal audit of the ship within three months;

.4 the master and officers are familiar with the safety management system and the planned arrangements for its implementation;

.5 instructions, which have been identified as being essential, are provided prior to sailing; and

.6 relevant information on the safety management system has been given in a working language or languages understood by the ship's personnel.

15 VERIFICATION

15.1 All verifications required by the provisions of this Code should be carried out in accordance with procedures acceptable to the Administration, taking into account the guidelines developed by the Organization.*

16 FORMS OF CERTIFICATES

16.1 The Document of Compliance, the Safety Management Certificate, the Interim Document of Compliance and the Interim Safety Management Certificate should be drawn up in a form corresponding to the models given in the appendix to this Code. If the language used is neither English nor French, the text should include a translation into one of these languages.

16.2 In addition to the requirements of paragraph 13.3, the ship types indicated on the Document of Compliance and the Interim Document of Compliance may be endorsed to reflect any limitations in the operations of the ships described in the safety management system.

---

* Refer to the Guidelines on implementation of the International Safety Management (ISM) Code by Administrations, adopted by the Organization by resolution A.1022(26) (see page 33 of this publication).

Appendix

Forms of the Document of Compliance, the Safety Management Certificate, the Interim Document of Compliance and the Interim Safety Management Certificate

DOCUMENT OF COMPLIANCE

(Official seal)   *(State)*

Certificate No.

Issued under the provisions of the
INTERNATIONAL CONVENTION FOR THE SAFETY OF LIFE AT SEA, 1974,
as amended

Under the authority of the Government of . . . .
(name of the State)

by . . . .
(person or organization authorized)

Name and address of the Company . . . .

. . . .
(see paragraph 1.1.2 of the ISM Code)

Company identification number . . . .

THIS IS TO CERTIFY THAT the safety management system of the Company has been audited and that it complies with the requirements of the International Management Code for the Safe Operation of Ships and for Pollution Prevention (ISM Code) for the types of ships listed below (delete as appropriate):

> Passenger ship
> Passenger high-speed craft
> Cargo high-speed craft
> Bulk carrier
> Oil tanker
> Chemical tanker
> Gas carrier
> Mobile offshore drilling unit
> Other cargo ship

This Document of Compliance is valid until . . . . subject to periodical verification.

Completion date of the verification on which this certificate is based . . . .

(dd/mm/yyyy)

Issued at . . . .

(Place of issue of the Document)

Date of issue . . . .

(Signature of the duly authorized official issuing the Document)

(Seal or stamp of issuing authority, as appropriate)

Certificate No.

ENDORSEMENT FOR ANNUAL VERIFICATION

THIS IS TO CERTIFY THAT, at the periodical verification in accordance with regulation IX/6.1 of the Convention and paragraph 13.4 of the ISM Code, the safety management system was found to comply with the requirements of the ISM Code.

1st ANNUAL VERIFICATION Signed: . . . .
                (Signature of authorized official)

                Place: . . . .

                Date: . . . .

2nd ANNUAL VERIFICATION Signed: . . . .
                (Signature of authorized official)

                Place: . . . .

                Date: . . . .

3rd ANNUAL VERIFICATION Signed: . . . .
                (Signature of authorized official)

                Place: . . . .

                Date: . . . .

4th ANNUAL VERIFICATION Signed: . . . .
                (Signature of authorized official)

                Place: . . . .

                Date: . . . .

SAFETY MANAGEMENT CERTIFICATE

(Official seal) *(State)*

Certificate No.

Issued under the provisions of the
INTERNATIONAL CONVENTION FOR THE SAFETY OF LIFE AT SEA, 1974,
as amended

Under the authority of the Government of ....
(name of the State)

by ....
(person or organization authorized)

Name of ship: ....

Distinctive number or letters: ....

Port of registry: ....

Type of ship:* ....

Gross tonnage: ....

IMO Number: ....

Name and address of the Company: ....

....
(see paragraph 1.1.2 of the ISM Code)

Company identification number ....

THIS IS TO CERTIFY THAT the safety management system of the ship has been audited and that it complies with the requirements of the International Management Code for the Safe Operation of Ships and for Pollution Prevention (ISM Code), following verification that the Document of Compliance for the Company is applicable to this type of ship.

---

* Insert the type of ship from among the following: passenger ship; passenger high-speed craft; cargo high-speed craft; bulk carrier; oil tanker; chemical tanker; gas carrier; mobile offshore drilling unit; other cargo ship.

This Safety Management Certificate is valid until . . . . , subject
to periodical verification and the Document of Compliance remaining valid.

Completion date of the verification on which this certificate is based . . . .
(dd/mm/yyyy)

Issued at . . . .
(Place of issue of the Certificate)

Date of issue . . . .
                                        (Signature of the duly authorized
                                        official issuing the Certificate)

(Seal or stamp of the authority, as appropriate)

27

Certificate No.

ENDORSEMENT FOR INTERMEDIATE VERIFICATION AND ADDITIONAL VERIFICATION (IF REQUIRED)

THIS IS TO CERTIFY THAT, at the periodical verification in accordance with regulation IX/6.1 of the Convention and paragraph 13.8 of the ISM Code, the safety management system was found to comply with the requirements of the ISM Code.

INTERMEDIATE VERIFICATION
(to be completed between
the second and third
anniversary dates)

Signed: . . . .
(Signature of authorized official)

Place: . . . .

Date: . . . .

ADDITIONAL VERIFICATION*

Signed: . . . .
(Signature of authorized official)

Place: . . . .

Date: . . . .

ADDITIONAL VERIFICATION*

Signed: . . . .
(Signature of authorized official)

Place: . . . .

Date: . . . .

ADDITIONAL VERIFICATION*

Signed: . . . .
(Signature of authorized official)

Place: . . . .

Date: . . . .

---

* If applicable. Reference is made to the relevant provisions of section 3.2 "Initial verification" of the Guidelines on implementation of the International Safety Management (ISM) Code by Administrations adopted by the Organization by resolution A.1022(26) (see page 33 of this publication).

Certificate No.

ENDORSEMENT WHERE THE RENEWAL VERIFICATION HAS BEEN COMPLETED AND PART B 13.13 OF THE ISM CODE APPLIES

The ship complies with the relevant provisions of part B of the ISM Code, and the Certificate should, in accordance with part B 13.13 of the ISM Code, be accepted as valid until . . . .

Signed: . . . .
(Signature of authorized official)

Place: . . . .

Date: . . . .

(Seal or stamp of the authority, as appropriate)

ENDORSEMENT TO EXTEND THE VALIDITY OF THE CERTIFICATE UNTIL REACHING THE PORT OF VERIFICATION WHERE PART B 13.12 OF THE ISM CODE APPLIES OR FOR A PERIOD OF GRACE WHERE PART B 13.14 OF THE ISM CODE APPLIES

This Certificate should, in accordance with part B 13.12 or part B 13.14 of the ISM Code, be accepted as valid until . . . .

Signed: . . . .
(Signature of authorized official)

Place: . . . .

Date: . . . .

(Seal or stamp of the authority, as appropriate)

INTERIM DOCUMENT OF COMPLIANCE

(Official seal)   *(State)*

Certificate No.

Issued under the provisions of the
INTERNATIONAL CONVENTION FOR THE SAFETY OF LIFE AT SEA, 1974,
as amended

Under the authority of the Government of ....
(name of the State)

by ....
(person or organization authorized)

Name and address of the Company ....

....
(see paragraph 1.1.2 of the ISM Code)

Company identification number ....

THIS IS TO CERTIFY THAT the safety management system of the Company has been recognized as meeting the objectives of paragraph 1.2.3 of the International Management Code for the Safe Operation of Ships and for Pollution Prevention (ISM Code) for the types of ships listed below (delete as appropriate):

> Passenger ship
> Passenger high-speed craft
> Cargo high-speed craft
> Bulk carrier
> Oil tanker
> Chemical tanker
> Gas carrier
> Mobile offshore drilling unit
> Other cargo ship

This Interim Document of Compliance is valid until ....

Issued at ....
(Place of issue of the Document)

Date of issue ....
       (dd/mm/yyyy)   *(Signature of the duly authorized official issuing the Document)*

(Seal or stamp of the authority, as appropriate)

INTERIM SAFETY MANAGEMENT CERTIFICATE

(Official seal)   *(State)*

Certificate No.

Issued under the provisions of the
INTERNATIONAL CONVENTION FOR THE SAFETY OF LIFE AT SEA, 1974,
as amended

Under the authority of the Government of . . . .
(name of the State)

by . . . .
(person or organization authorized)

Name of ship: . . . .

Distinctive number or letters: . . . .

Port of registry: . . . .

Type of ship:* . . . .

Gross tonnage: . . . .

IMO Number: . . . .

Name and address of the Company: . . . .

. . . .
(see paragraph 1.1.2 of the ISM Code)

Company identification number . . . .

THIS IS TO CERTIFY THAT the requirements of paragraph 14.4 of the ISM Code have been met and that the Document of Compliance/Interim Document of Compliance† of the Company is relevant to this ship.

This Interim Safety Management Certificate is valid until . . . . subject to the Document of Compliance/Interim Document of Compliance† remaining valid.

---

* Insert the type of ship from among the following: passenger ship; passenger high-speed craft; cargo high-speed craft; bulk carrier; oil tanker; chemical tanker; gas carrier; mobile offshore drilling unit; other cargo ship.

† Delete as appropriate.

Issued at . . . .
(Place of issue of the Certificate)

Date of issue . . . .
(Signature of the duly authorized
official issuing the Certificate)

(Seal or stamp of the authority, as appropriate)

The validity of this Interim Safety Management Certificate
is extended to . . . .
Date of extension . . . .
(Signature of the duly authorized
official extending the validity)

(Seal or stamp of issuing authority, as appropriate)

Guidelines on implementation of the International Safety Management Code by Administrations

Guidelines on implementation of the International Safety Management (ISM) Code by Administrations

Resolution A.1022(26)

INTRODUCTION

The ISM Code

The International Management Code for the Safe Operation of Ships and for Pollution Prevention (International Safety Management (ISM) Code) was adopted by the Organization by resolution A.741(18) and became mandatory by virtue of the entry into force on 1 July 1998 of SOLAS chapter IX on Management for the Safe Operation of Ships. The ISM Code provides an international standard for the safe management and operation of ships and for pollution prevention.

The Maritime Safety Committee, at its eighty-fifth session, adopted amendments to sections 1, 5, 7, 8, 9, 10, 12, 13, 14 and the appendix of the ISM Code by resolution MSC.273(85). As a result it is necessary to revise the Guidelines contained in Assembly resolution A.913(22), which is being superseded by the present Guidelines.

The ISM Code requires that Companies establish safety objectives as described in section 1.2 of the ISM Code, and in addition that the Companies develop, implement and maintain a safety management system which includes functional requirements as listed in section 1.4 of the ISM Code.

The application of the ISM Code should *support and encourage* the development of a safety culture in shipping. Success factors for the development of a safety culture are, *inter alia*, commitment, values and beliefs.

Mandatory application of the ISM Code

Appropriate organization of management, ashore and on board, is needed to ensure adequate standards of safety and pollution prevention. A systematic approach to management by those responsible for management of ships is therefore required. The objectives of the mandatory application of the ISM Code are to ensure:

.1   compliance with mandatory rules and regulations related to the safe operation of ships and protection of the environment; and

.2   the effective implementation and enforcement thereof by Administrations.

Effective enforcement by Administrations must include verification that the safety management system complies with the requirements as stipulated in the ISM Code, as well as verification of compliance with mandatory rules and regulations.

The mandatory application of the ISM Code should ensure, support and encourage the taking into account of applicable codes, guidelines and standards recommended by the Organization, Administrations, classification societies and maritime industry organizations.

Verification and certification responsibilities

The Administration is responsible for verifying compliance with the requirements of the ISM Code and for issuing Documents of Compliance to Companies and Safety Management Certificates to ships.

Resolutions A.739(18) – Guidelines for the authorization of organizations acting on behalf of the Administration and A.789(19) – Specifications on the survey and certification functions of recognized organizations acting on behalf of the Administration, which have been made mandatory by virtue of SOLAS regulation XI/1, and resolution A.847(20) – Guidelines to assist flag States in the implementation of IMO instruments,[*] are applicable when Administrations authorize organizations to issue Documents of Compliance and Safety Management Certificates on their behalf.

---

[*] Resolution A.847(20) has been superseded by resolution A.996(25), Code for the Implementation of Mandatory IMO Instruments, 2007, as amended by resolution A.1019(26).

1   SCOPE AND APPLICATION

1.1   Definitions

The terms used in these Guidelines have the same meaning as those given in the ISM Code.

1.2   Scope and application

1.2.1   These Guidelines establish basic principles:

.1   for verifying that the safety management system of a Company responsible for the operation of ships, or the safety management system for the ship or ships controlled by the Company, complies with the ISM Code; and

.2   for the issue and annual verification of the Document of Compliance and for the issue and intermediate verification of the Safety Management Certificate.

2   VERIFYING COMPLIANCE WITH THE ISM CODE

2.1   General

2.1.1   To comply with the requirements of the ISM Code, Companies should develop, implement and maintain a safety management system to ensure that the safety and environmental protection policy of the Company is implemented. The Company policy should include the objectives defined by the ISM Code.*

2.1.2   Administrations should verify compliance with the requirements of the ISM Code by determining:

.1   the conformity of the Company's safety management system with the requirements of the ISM Code; and

.2   that the safety management system ensures that the objectives defined in paragraph 1.2.3 of the ISM Code are met.

---

* The ICS/ISF Guidelines on the application of the IMO International Safety Management Code provide useful guidance on important individual elements of a safety management system and its development by Companies.

2.1.3 Determining the conformity or non-conformity of safety management system elements with the requirements specified by the ISM Code may demand that criteria for assessment be developed. Administrations are recommended to limit the development of criteria in the form of prescriptive management system solutions. Criteria for assessment in the form of prescriptive requirements may have the effect that safety management in shipping results in Companies implementing solutions prepared by others, and it may then be difficult for a Company to develop the solutions which best suit that particular Company, operation or ship.

2.1.4 Therefore, Administrations are recommended to ensure that these assessments are based on determining the effectiveness of the safety management system in meeting specified objectives, rather than conformity with detailed requirements in addition to those contained in the ISM Code, so as to reduce the need for developing criteria to facilitate assessment of the Companies' compliance with the Code.

2.2 The ability of the safety management system to meet general safety management objectives

2.2.1 The ISM Code identifies general safety management objectives. These objectives are:

.1 to provide for safe practices in ship operation and a safe working environment;

.2 to assess all identified risks to its ships, personnel and the environment and establish appropriate safeguards; and

.3 to improve continuously the safety-management skills of personnel ashore and aboard, including preparing for emergencies related both to safety and to environmental protection.

The verification should support and encourage Companies in achieving these objectives.

2.2.2 These objectives provide clear guidance to Companies for the development of safety management system elements in compliance with the ISM Code. Since, however, the ability of the safety management system to achieve these objectives cannot be determined beyond whether the safety management system complies with the requirements of the ISM Code, they should not form the basis for establishing detailed interpretations to be used for determining conformity or non-conformity with the requirements of the ISM Code.

2.3 The ability of the safety management system to meet specific requirements of safety and pollution prevention

2.3.1 The main criterion which should govern the development of inter-pretations needed for assessing compliance with the requirements of the ISM Code should be the ability of the safety management system to meet the specific requirements defined by the ISM Code in terms of specific standards of safety and pollution prevention.

The specific standards of safety and protection of the environment speci-fied by the ISM Code are:

> **.1** compliance with mandatory rules and regulations; and

> **.2** that applicable codes, guidelines and standards recom-mended by the Organization, Administrations, classification societies and other maritime industry organizations are taken into account.

2.3.2 All records having the potential to facilitate verification of compliance with the ISM Code should be open to scrutiny during an examination. For this purpose the Administration should ensure that the Company provides auditors with statutory and classification records relevant to the actions taken by the Company to ensure that compliance with mandatory rules and regulations is maintained. In this regard the records may be examined to substantiate their authenticity and veracity.

2.3.3 Some mandatory requirements may not be subject to statutory or classification surveys, such as:

> **.1** maintaining the condition of ship and equipment between surveys; and

> **.2** certain operational requirements.

Specific arrangements may be required to ensure compliance and to provide for the objective evidence needed for verification in these cases, such as:

.1 documented procedures and instructions; and

.2 documentation of the verification carried out by senior officers of day-to-day operation when relevant to ensure compliance.

2.3.4 The verification of compliance with mandatory rules and regulations, which is part of the ISM Code certification, neither duplicates nor substitutes surveys for other maritime certificates. The verification of compliance with the ISM Code does not relieve the Company, the master or any other entity or person involved in the management or operation of the ship of their responsibilities.

2.3.5 Administrations should ensure that the Company has:

.1 taken into account the recommendations, as referred to in 1.2.3.2 of the ISM Code, when establishing the safety management system; and

.2 developed procedures to ensure that these recommendations are implemented on shore and on board.

2.3.6 Within a safety management system, implementation of codes, guidelines and standards recommended by the Organization, Administrations, classification societies and other maritime industry organizations does not make these recommendations mandatory under the ISM Code. Nevertheless auditors should encourage Companies to adopt these recommendations whenever applicable to the Company.

3 THE CERTIFICATION PROCESS

3.1 Certification activities

3.1.1 The certification process relevant to a Document of Compliance for a Company and a Safety Management Certificate to a ship will normally involve the following steps:

.1 initial verification;

.2 annual or intermediate verification;

> **.3** renewal verification; and
>
> **.4** additional verification.

These verifications are carried out at the request of the Company to the Administration, or to the organization recognized by the Administration to perform certification functions under the ISM Code, or at the request of the Administration by another Contracting Government to the Convention.

The verifications will include an audit of the safety management system.

3.2 Initial verification

3.2.1 The Company should apply for ISM Code certification to the Administration.

3.2.2 An assessment of the shoreside management system undertaken by the Administration would necessitate assessment of the offices where such management is carried out and possibly of other locations, depending on the Company's organization and the functions of the various locations.

3.2.3 On satisfactory completion of the assessment of the shoreside safety management system, arrangements/planning may commence for the assessment of the Company's ships.

3.2.4 On satisfactory completion of the assessment, a Document of Compliance will be issued to the Company, copies of which should be forwarded to each shoreside premises and each ship in the Company's fleet. As each ship is assessed and issued with a Safety Management Certificate, a copy of it should also be forwarded to the Company's head office.

3.2.5 In cases where certificates are issued by a recognized organization, copies of all certificates should also be sent to the Administration.

3.2.6 The safety management audit for the Company and for a ship will involve the same basic steps. The purpose is to verify that a Company or a ship complies with the requirements of the ISM Code. The audits include:

> **.1** the conformity of the Company's safety management system with the requirements of the ISM Code, including objective

evidence demonstrating that the Company's safety management system has been in operation for at least three months and that a safety management system has been in operation on board at least one ship of each type operated by the Company for at least three months; and

.2 that the safety management system ensures that the objectives defined in paragraph 1.2.3 of the ISM Code are met. This includes verification that the Document of Compliance for the Company responsible for the operation of the ship is applicable to that particular type of ship, and assessment of the shipboard safety management system to verify that it complies with the requirements of the ISM Code, and that it is implemented. Objective evidence demonstrating that the Company's safety management system has been functioning effectively for at least three months on board the ship and ashore should be available, including, *inter alia*, records from the internal audit performed by the Company.

3.3 Annual verification of Document of Compliance

3.3.1 Annual safety management audits are to be carried out to maintain the validity of the Document of Compliance, and should include examining and verifying the correctness of the statutory and classification records presented for at least one ship of each type to which the Document of Compliance applies. The purpose of these audits is to verify the effective functioning of the safety management system, and that any modifications made to the safety management system comply with the requirements of the ISM Code.

3.3.2 Annual verification is to be carried out within three months before and after each anniversary date of the Document of Compliance. A schedule not exceeding three months is to be agreed for completion of the necessary corrective actions.

3.3.3 Where the Company has more than one shoreside premises, each of which may not have been visited at the initial assessment, the annual assessments should endeavour to ensure that all sites are visited during the period of validity of the Document of Compliance.

3.4 Intermediate verification of Safety Management Certificates

3.4.1 Intermediate safety management audits should be carried out to maintain the validity of the Safety Management Certificate. The purpose of these audits is to verify the effective functioning of the safety management system and that any modifications made to the safety management system comply with the requirements of the ISM Code. In certain cases, particularly during the initial period of operation under the safety management system, the Administration may find it necessary to increase the frequency of the intermediate verification. Additionally, the nature of non-conformities may also provide a basis for increasing the frequency of intermediate verifications.

3.4.2 If only one intermediate verification is to be carried out, it should take place between the second and third anniversary date of the issue of the Safety Management Certificate.

3.5 Renewal verification

Renewal verifications are to be performed before the validity of the Document of Compliance or the Safety Management Certificate expires. The renewal verification will address all the elements of the safety management system and the activities to which the requirements of the ISM Code apply. Renewal verification may be carried out from three months before the date of expiry of the Document of Compliance or the Safety Management Certificate, and should be completed before their date of expiry.

3.6 Safety management audits

The procedure for safety management audits outlined in the following paragraphs includes all steps relevant for initial verification. Safety management audits for annual verification and renewal verification should be based on the same principles even if their scope may be different.

3.7 Application for audit

3.7.1 The Company should submit a request for audit to the Administration or to the organization recognized by the Administration for issuing a Document of Compliance or a Safety Management Certificate on behalf of the Administration.

3.7.2 The Administration or the recognized organization should then nominate the lead auditor and, if relevant, the audit team.

3.8   Preliminary review (Document review)

As a basis for planning the audit, the auditor should review the safety management manual to determine the adequacy of the safety management system in meeting the requirements of the ISM Code. If this review reveals that the system is not adequate, the audit will have to be delayed until the Company undertakes corrective action.

3.9   Preparing the audit

3.9.1 The nominated lead auditor should liaise with the Company and produce an audit plan.

3.9.2 The auditor should provide the working documents which are to govern the execution of the audit to facilitate the assessments, investigations and examinations in accordance with the standard procedures, instructions and forms which have been established to ensure consistent auditing practices.

3.9.3 The audit team should be able to communicate effectively with auditees.

3.10   Executing the audit

3.10.1 The audit should start with an opening meeting in order to introduce the audit team to the Company's senior management, summarize the methods for conducting the audit, confirm that all agreed facilities are available, confirm time and date for a closing meeting and clarify possible unclear details relevant to the audit.

3.10.2 The audit team should assess the safety management system on the basis of the documentation presented by the Company and objective evidence as to its effective implementation.

3.10.3 Evidence should be collected through interviews and examination of documents. Observation of activities and conditions may also be included when necessary to determine the effectiveness of the safety management system in meeting the specific standards of safety and protection of the environment required by the ISM Code.

3.10.4 Audit observations should be documented. After activities have been audited, the audit team should review their observations to determine which are to be reported as non-conformities. Non-conformities should be reported in terms of the general and specific provisions of the ISM Code.

3.10.5 At the end of the audit, prior to preparing the audit report, the audit team should hold a meeting with the senior management of the Company and those responsible for the functions concerned. The purpose is to present the observations in such a way as to ensure that the results of the audit are clearly understood.

3.11 Audit report

3.11.1 The audit report should be prepared under the direction of the lead auditor, who is responsible for its accuracy and completeness.

3.11.2 The audit report should include the audit plan, identification of audit team members, dates and identification of the Company, observations on any non-conformities and observations on the effectiveness of the safety management system in meeting the specified objectives.

3.11.3 The Company should receive a copy of the audit report. The Company should be advised to provide a copy of the shipboard audit reports to the ship.

3.12 Corrective action follow-up

3.12.1 The Company is responsible for determining and initiating the corrective action needed to correct a non-conformity or to correct the cause of the non-conformity. Failure to correct non-conformities with specific requirements of the ISM Code may affect the validity of the Document of Compliance and related Safety Management Certificates.

3.12.2 Corrective actions and possible subsequent follow-up audits should be completed within the time period agreed. The Company should apply for the follow-up audits.

3.13 Company responsibilities pertaining to safety management audits

3.13.1 The verification of compliance with the requirements of the ISM Code does not relieve the Company, management, officers or seafarers of their obligations as to compliance with national and international legislation related to safety and protection of the environment.

3.13.2 The Company is responsible for:

.1 informing relevant employees about the objectives and scope of the ISM Code certification;

.2 appointing responsible members of staff to accompany members of the team performing the certification;

.3 providing the resources needed by those performing the certification to ensure an effective and efficient verification process;

.4 providing access and evidential material as requested by those performing the certification; and

.5 co-operating with the verification team to permit the certification objectives to be achieved.

3.13.3 Where major non-conformities are identified, Administrations and recognized organizations (ROs) should comply with the procedures stated in MSC/Circ.1059 – MEPC/Circ.401.

3.14 Responsibilities of the organization performing the ISM Code certification

The organization performing the ISM Code certification is responsible for ensuring that the certification process is performed according to the ISM Code and these Guidelines. This includes management control of all aspects of the certification according to the appendix to these Guidelines.

3.15   Responsibilities of the verification team

3.15.1 Whether the verifications involved with certification are performed by a team or not, one person should be in charge of the verification. The leader should be given the authority to make final decisions regarding the conduct of the verification and any observations. His responsibilities should include:

.1   preparation of a plan for the verification; and

.2   submission of the report of the verification.

3.15.2 Personnel participating in the verification are responsible for complying with the requirements governing the verification, ensuring confidentiality of documents pertaining to the certification and treating privileged information with discretion.

Appendix

Standards on ISM Code certification arrangements

1   Introduction

The audit team involved with ISM Code certification, and the organization under which it may be managed, should comply with the specific requirements stated in this annex.

2   Standard of management

2.1 Organizations managing verification of compliance with the ISM Code should have, in their own organization, competence in relation to:

  .1   ensuring compliance with the rules and regulations, including certification of seafarers, for the ships operated by the Company;

  .2   approval, survey and certification activities;

  .3   the terms of reference that must be taken into account under the safety management system as required by the ISM Code; and

  .4   practical experience of ship operation.

2.2 The Convention requires that organizations recognized by Administrations for issuing a Document of Compliance and a Safety Management Certificate at their request should comply with resolutions A.739(18) – Guidelines for the authorization of organizations acting on behalf of the Administration[*] and A.789(19) – Specifications on the survey and certification functions of recognized organizations acting on behalf of the Administration.

2.3 Any organization performing verification of compliance with the provisions of the ISM Code should ensure that there exists independence between the personnel providing consultancy services and those involved in the certification procedure.

---

[*] As amended by resolution MSC.208(81).

3   Standards of competence

3.1   *ISM Code certification scheme management*

Management of ISM Code certification schemes should be carried out by those who have practical knowledge of ISM Code certification procedures and practices.

3.2   *Basic competence for performing verification*

3.2.1   Personnel who are to participate in the verification of compliance with the requirements of the ISM Code should have a minimum of formal education comprising the following:

.1   qualifications from a tertiary institution recognized by the Administration or by the recognized organization within a relevant field of engineering or physical science (minimum two-year programme); or

.2   qualifications from a marine or nautical institution and relevant seagoing experience as a certified ship officer.

3.2.2   They should have undergone training to ensure adequate competence and skills for performing verification of compliance with the requirements of the ISM Code, particularly with regard to:

.1   knowledge and understanding of the ISM Code;

.2   mandatory rules and regulations;

.3   the terms of reference which the ISM Code requires that Companies should take into account;

.4   assessment techniques of examining, questioning, evaluating and reporting;

.5   technical or operational aspects of safety management;

.6   basic knowledge of shipping and shipboard operations; and

.7   participation in at least one marine-related management system audit.

3.2.3 Such competence should be demonstrated through written or oral examinations, or other acceptable means.

3.3 *Competence for initial verification and renewal verification*

3.3.1 In order to assess fully whether the Company or the ship complies with the requirements of the ISM Code, in addition to the basic competence stated under 3.2 above, personnel who are to perform initial verifications or renewal verifications for a Document of Compliance or a Safety Management Certificate must possess the competence to:

> **.1** determine whether the safety management system elements conform or do not conform with the requirements of the ISM Code;
>
> **.2** determine the effectiveness of the Company's safety management system, or that of the ship, to ensure compliance with rules and regulations as evidenced by the statutory and classification survey records;
>
> **.3** assess the effectiveness of the safety management system in ensuring compliance with other rules and regulations which are not covered by statutory and classification surveys and enabling verification of compliance with these rules and regulations; and
>
> **.4** assess whether the safe practices recommended by the Organization, Administrations, classification societies and maritime industry organizations have been taken into account.

3.3.2 This competence can be accomplished by teams which together possess the total competence required.

3.3.3 Personnel who are to be in charge of initial verification or renewal verification of compliance with the requirements of the ISM Code should have at least five years' experience in areas relevant to the technical or operational aspects of safety management, and should have participated in at least three initial verifications or renewal verifications. Participation in verification of compliance with other management standards may be considered as equivalent to participation in verification of compliance with the ISM Code.

3.4 *Competence for annual, intermediate and interim verification*

Personnel who are to perform annual, intermediate and interim verifications should satisfy basic requirements for personnel participating in verifications and should have participated in a minimum of two annual, renewal or initial verifications. They should have received special instructions needed to ensure that they possess the competence required to determine the effectiveness of the Company's safety management system.

4   Qualification arrangements

Organizations performing ISM Code certification should have implemented a documented system for qualification and continuous updating of the knowledge and competence of personnel who are to perform verification of compliance with the ISM Code. This system should comprise theoretical training courses covering all the competence requirements and the appropriate procedures connected to the certification process, as well as practical tutored training, and it should provide documented evidence of satisfactory completion of the training.

5   Certification procedures and instructions

Organizations performing ISM Code certification should have implemented a documented system to ensure that the certification process is performed in accordance with this standard. This system should, *inter alia*, include procedures and instructions for the following:

.1   contractual agreements with Companies;

.2   planning, scheduling and performing verification;

.3   reporting results from verification;

.4   issue of Documents of Compliance, Safety Management Certificates and Interim Documents of Compliance and Safety Management Certificates; and

.5   corrective action and follow-up of verifications, including actions to be taken in cases of major non-conformity.

Guidelines for the operational implementation of the International Safety Management Code by Companies

Guidelines for the operational implementation of the International Safety Management (ISM) Code by Companies

Annex to MSC–MEPC.7/Circ.5

1 INTRODUCTION

1.1 The ISM Code

1.1.1 The International Management Code for the Safe Operation of Ships and for Pollution Prevention (International Safety Management (ISM) Code) was adopted by the Organization by resolution A.741(18) and became mandatory by virtue of the entry into force on 1 July 1998 of SOLAS chapter IX on Management for the Safe Operation of Ships. The ISM Code provides an international standard for the safe management and operation of ships and for pollution prevention.

1.1.2 The Maritime Safety Committee, at its seventy-third session, adopted amendments to chapter IX of SOLAS by resolution MSC.99(73), and to sections 1, 7, 13, 14, 15 and 16 of the ISM Code by resolution MSC.104(73).

1.1.3 The ISM Code requires that Companies establish safety objectives as described in section 1.2 of the ISM Code, and in addition that the Companies develop, implement and maintain a safety management system which includes functional requirements as listed in section 1.4 of the ISM Code.

1.1.4 The application of the ISM Code should *support and encourage* the development of a safety culture in shipping. Success factors for the development of a safety culture are, *inter alia*, commitment, values and beliefs.

2   SCOPE AND APPLICATION

2.1   Definitions

The terms used in these Guidelines have the same meaning as those given in the ISM Code.

2.2   Scope and application

2.2.1   These Guidelines establish the basic principles for:

    .1   reviewing the safety management system by a Company;

    .2   the role of the designated person under the ISM Code;

    .3   reporting and analysing of non-conformities, accidents and hazardous occurrences (including near misses); and

    .4   performing internal audits and management reviews,

and do not reduce or replace the Company's responsibilities outlined in the ISM Code.

3   DEVELOPMENT OF THE SAFETY MANAGEMENT SYSTEM

3.1   The ISM Code requires that Companies establish safety objectives as described in section 1.2 of the ISM Code, and in addition that Companies develop, implement and maintain a safety management system (SMS) which includes functional requirements as listed in section 1.4 of the ISM Code.

3.2   Given the self-regulatory principles of the ISM Code, the internal verification and review processes are key elements in the implementation of each SMS. The Company should consider the outcome of internal audits, internal SMS reviews and analysis of non-conformities, accidents and hazardous occurrences to enhance the effectiveness of operations and procedures within their SMS. To comply with the Code, the Company should:

    .1   designate a person or persons with direct access to the highest level of management who should monitor the safe operation of each ship (section 4);

.2 ensure that adequate resources and shore-based support are provided to enable the designated person or persons to carry out their functions (section 3.3);

.3 define and document the master's responsibility with regard to reviewing the safety management system and reporting its deficiencies to the shore-based management (section 5.1);

.4 establish procedures for reporting and analysis of non-conformities, accidents and hazardous occurrences (section 9.1);

.5 periodically evaluate the effectiveness of, and when needed, review, the safety management system (section 12.2); and

.6 perform internal audits to verify whether safety management activities comply with the requirements of the safety management system (section 12.1).

4   DESIGNATED PERSON

4.1   A key role, as identified by the ISM Code, in the effective implementation of a safety management system is that of the designated person. This is the person based ashore whose influence and responsibilities should significantly affect the development and implementation of a safety culture within the Company.

4.2   The designated person should verify and monitor all safety and pollution prevention activities in the operation of each ship. This monitoring should include, at least, the following internal processes:

.1 communication and implementation of the safety and environmental protection policy;

.2 evaluation and review of the effectiveness of the safety management system;

.3 reporting and analysis of non-conformities, accidents and hazardous occurrences;

.4 organizing and monitoring of internal audits;

.5 appropriate revisions to the SMS; and

.6 ensuring that adequate resources and shore-based support are provided.

4.3   To enable the designated person to carry out this role effectively, the Company should provide adequate resources and shore-based support. These include:

   .1   personnel resources;

   .2   material resources;

   .3   any training required;

   .4   clearly defined and documented responsibility and authority; and

   .5   authority for reporting non-conformities and observations to the highest level of management.

4.4   Designated person(s) should have the qualifications, training and experience as set out in MSC–MEPC.7/Circ.6,[*] to effectively verify and monitor the implementation of the safety management system in compliance with the ISM Code.

5   REVIEW OF THE SAFETY MANAGEMENT SYSTEM

5.1   The Company should, when needed, review and evaluate the effectiveness of the SMS in accordance with procedures established by the company. Further, it is one of the master's responsibilities to review the safety management system and to report its deficiencies to the shore-based management. Shore-based and shipboard internal audits should be performed at least once a year.

5.2   Management reviews support companies' efforts in achieving the general safety management objectives as defined in section 1.2.2 of the ISM Code. Based upon the results of such reviews, the Company should implement measures to improve further the effectiveness of the system. The review should be performed on a periodical basis or when needed, e.g., in case of serious system failures. Any deficiencies found during the management review should be provided with appropriate corrective action taking into account the Company's objectives. The results of such reviews should be brought to the attention of all personnel involved in

---

* See page 61 of this publication.

a formal way. The management review should at least take into account the results of the internal audits, any non-conformities reported by the personnel, the master's reviews, analysis of non-conformities, accidents and hazardous occurrences and any other evidence of possible failure of the SMS, like non-conformities by external parties, PSC inspection reports, etc.

6 REPORTING AND ANALYSING OF NON-CONFORMITIES, OBSERVATIONS, ACCIDENTS AND HAZARDOUS OCCURRENCES

6.1 The SMS should contain procedures to ensure that non-conformities, observations and hazardous occurrences are reported to the responsible person of the management. The Company should have a system in place for recording, investigating, evaluating, reviewing and analysing such reports, and to take action as appropriate.

6.2 The system should ensure such reports are reviewed and evaluated by the responsible person(s) in order to determine appropriate corrective action and to ensure that recurrences are avoided. The evaluation of reports may result in:

   .1   appropriate corrective actions;

   .2   amendments to existing procedures and instructions; and

   .3   development of new procedures and instructions.

6.3 The responsible person should properly monitor the follow-up and closing-out of the non-conformities/deficiency reports. The receipt of reports should be acknowledged to those persons who have raised the reports. This should include the status of the report and any decisions made.

6.4 The Company should encourage the reporting of near misses to maintain and improve safety awareness (see MSC/Circ.1015). A near miss can be defined as hazardous situation where an accident was avoided. The reporting and analysis of such incidents are essential for an effective risk assessment by the Company, especially where accident information is not available.

7   INTERNAL AUDITS

7.1   Companies should carry out internal audits at least once per year to verify whether shore-based and shipboard activities comply with the SMS. These internal verifications should be prepared and conducted in accordance with procedures established by the Company. The procedures should at least consider the following elements:

.1   responsibilities;

.2   competence and selection of auditors;

.3   audit scheduling;

.4   preparing and planning the audit;

.5   executing the audit;

.6   audit report; and

.7   corrective action follow-up.

8   QUALIFICATIONS, TRAINING AND EXPERIENCE

8.1   The ISM Code requires the Company to ensure that all personnel involved in the Company's SMS have an adequate understanding of relevant rules, regulations, codes and guidelines. The Company should ensure that all personnel have the qualifications, training and experience that may be required in support of the SMS.

Guidance on the qualifications, training and experience necessary for undertaking the role of the designated person under the provisions of the International Safety Management Code

Guidance on the qualifications, training and experience necessary for undertaking the role of the designated person under the provisions of the International Safety Management (ISM) Code

Annex to MSC–MEPC.7/Circ.6

1   INTRODUCTION

The present Guidance applies to persons undertaking the role of the designated person under the provisions of the International Safety Management (ISM) Code.

2   QUALIFICATIONS

2.1   Designated person should have a minimum of formal education as follows:

    .1   qualifications from a tertiary institution recognized by the Administration or by the recognized organization, within a relevant field of management, engineering or physical science, or

    .2   qualifications and seagoing experience as a certified ship officer pursuant to the International Convention on Standards of Training, Certification and Watchkeeping for Seafarers (STCW), 1978, as amended, or

    .3   other formal education combined with not less than three years' practical senior level experience in ship management operations.

3 TRAINING

3.1 Designated person should have undergone training relating to safety management elements in compliance with the requirements of the ISM Code, particularly with regard to:

.1 knowledge and understanding of the ISM Code;

.2 mandatory rules and regulations;

.3 applicable codes, guidelines and standards as appropriate;

.4 assessment techniques of examining, questioning, evaluating and reporting;

.5 technical or operational aspects of safety management;

.6 appropriate knowledge of shipping and shipboard operations;

.7 participation in at least one marine-related management system audit; and

.8 effective communications with shipboard staff and senior management.

4 EXPERIENCE

4.1 Designated person should have experience to:

.1 present ISM matters to the highest level of management and gain sustained support for safety management system improvements;

.2 determine whether the safety management system elements meet the requirements of the ISM Code;

.3 determine the effectiveness of the safety management system within the Company and the ship by using established principles of internal audit and management review to ensure compliance with rules and regulations;

.4   assess the effectiveness of the safety management system in ensuring compliance with other rules and regulations which are not covered by statutory and classification surveys and enabling verification of compliance with these rules and regulations;

.5   assess whether the safe practices recommended by the Organization, Administrations, classification societies, other international bodies and maritime industry organizations to promote a safety culture had been taken into account; and

.6   gather and analyse data from hazardous occurrences, hazardous situations, near misses, incidents and accidents and apply the lessons learnt to improve the safety management system within the Company and its ships.

5   COMPANY REQUIREMENTS AND RECORDS

5.1   The Company should provide training courses covering qualification, training and experience and the appropriate procedures connected to compliance with the ISM Code including practical training and continuous updating. The Company should also provide documentary evidence that the designated person has the relevant qualification, training and experience to undertake the duties under the provisions of the ISM Code.

Guidance on near-miss reporting

Guidance on near-miss reporting

Annex to MSC–MEPC.7/Circ.7

1   INTRODUCTION

1.1   Companies should investigate near misses as a regulatory requirement under the "Hazardous Occurrences" part of the ISM Code. Aside from the fact that near-miss reporting is a requirement, it also makes good business and economic sense because it can improve vessel and crew performance and, in many cases, reduce costs. Investigating near misses is an integral component of continuous improvement in safety management systems. This benefit can only be achieved when seafarers are assured that such reporting will not result in punitive measures. Learning the lessons from near misses should help to improve safety performance since near misses can share the same underlying causes as losses.

1.2   For a company to realize the fullest potential benefits of near-miss reporting, seafarers and onshore employees need to understand the definition of a near miss to ensure that all near misses are reported. The company also needs to be clear about how the person who reports the near miss and those persons involved will be treated. The guidance that follows suggests that the company should encourage near-miss reporting and investigation by adopting a "just culture" approach.

1.3   A "just culture" features an atmosphere of responsible behaviour and trust whereby people are encouraged to provide essential safety-related information without fear of retribution. However, a distinction is drawn between acceptable and unacceptable behaviour. Unacceptable behaviour will not necessarily receive a guarantee that a person will not face consequences.

1.4   It is a crucial requirement that the company clearly define the circumstances in which it will guarantee a non-punitive outcome and confidentiality. The company should provide training and information about its approach to "just culture" near-miss reporting and investigation for all persons involved.

2   DEFINING NEAR MISS

2.1   Near miss: A sequence of events and/or conditions that could have resulted in loss. This loss was prevented only by a fortuitous break in the chain of events and/or conditions. The potential loss could be human injury, environmental damage, or negative business impact (e.g., repair or replacement costs, scheduling delays, contract violations, loss of reputation).

2.2   Some general examples of a near miss help to illustrate this definition:

.1   Any event that leads to the implementation of an emergency procedure, plan or response and thus prevents a loss. For example, a collision is narrowly avoided; or a crew member double checks a valve and discovers a wrong pressure reading on the supply side.

.2   Any event where an unexpected condition could lead to an adverse consequence, but which does not occur. For example, a person moves from a location immediately before a crane unexpectedly drops a load of cargo there; or a ship finds itself off course in normally shallow waters but does not ground because of an unusual high-spring tide.

.3   Any dangerous or hazardous situation or condition that is not discovered until after the danger has passed. For example, a vessel safely departs a port of call and discovers several hours into the voyage that the ship's radio was not tuned to the Harbour Master's radio frequency; or it is discovered that ECDIS display's scale does not match the scale, projection, or orientation of the chart and radar images.

3   OVERCOMING BARRIERS TO REPORTING NEAR MISSES

3.1   There are many barriers related to the reporting of near misses. In many cases, near misses are only known by the individual(s) involved who chose to report or not report the incident. Some of the main barriers to the reporting of near misses include the fear of being blamed, disciplined, embarrassed, or found legally liable. These are more prevalent in an organization that has a blame-oriented culture. Amongst other barriers are unsupportive company management attitudes such as complacency about known deficiencies; insincerity about addressing safety issues and discouragement of the reporting of near misses by demanding that seafarers conduct investigations in their own time.

3.2 These barriers can be overcome by management initiatives such as:

.1 Encouraging a "just culture" in the company which covers near-miss reporting.

.2 Assuring confidentiality for reporting near misses, both through company policy and by "sanitizing" analyses and reports so that personal information (information identifying an individual) of persons associated with a near miss is removed and remains confidential. Personal information should not be retained once the investigation and reporting processes are complete.

.3 Ensuring that investigations are adequately resourced.

.4 Following through on the near-miss report suggestions and recommendations. Once a decision has been made to implement, or not implement, the report's recommendations should be disseminated widely.

4 THE NEAR-MISS INVESTIGATION PROCESS

4.1 As a minimum, the following information should be gathered about any near miss:

.1 Who and what was involved?

.2 What happened, where, when, and in what sequence?

.3 What were the potential losses and their potential severity?

.4 What was the likelihood of a loss being realized?

.5 What is the likelihood of a recurrence of the chain of events and/or conditions that led to the near miss?

4.2   The answer to these questions will determine if an in-depth investigation is needed, or if a cursory report will suffice. An in-depth investigation is required of those near misses which are likely to recur and/or which could have had severe consequences.

4.3   Once a decision has been taken to proceed with a full investigation, further decisions are taken about levels of staffing required, who should be responsible, and what resources are required for the investigation to be completed successfully. The main steps in the investigation are:

Gathering near-miss information

4.4   Regardless of the nature of the near miss, the basic categories of data that should be gathered include: people, paper documents, electronic data, physical, and position/location. These data are vital for ensuring that an understanding can be reached about what, how, who, and eventually why the near miss occurred. Data gathering is done by interviews of key personnel and the collection of physical, position and location data, using such things as photographs, VDR recordings, charts, logs, or any damaged components. Furthermore, information should be gathered regarding safeguards in place to protect the persons on board and the public, and the operational systems impacting the near-miss event.

Analysing information

4.5   Applying data analysis techniques helps to identify information that still needs to be collected to resolve open questions about the near miss and its causes. This can make the collection of additional data more efficient. The end goal of this activity is to identify all causal factors.

Identifying causal factors

4.6   At this point the who, what, where, why, and when of the near miss is understood, and the human errors, structural/machinery/equipment/outfitting problems, and external factors that led to the near miss, have been identified. The next step is to better understand the causal factors that contributed to the near miss. There are a variety of identification methods for this purpose, including taxonomies of causes. These can be used for deep probing past the most evident causes.

Developing and implementing recommendations

4.7   Any recommendations made need to address all of the identified causal factors to improve organizational and shipboard policies, practices and procedures. Implementing appropriate recommendations is the key to eliminating or reducing the potential for the reoccurrence of similar near misses or more serious losses.

5   COMPLETING THE INVESTIGATION

5.1   Completion of the investigation process requires the generation of a report (either brief or extensive, depending on the depth of analysis performed and the extent of risk), and collating and storing the information in a way that supports subsequent (long-term) trend analysis.

5.2   The ultimate objective of near-miss reporting and investigating is to identify areas of concern and implement appropriate corrective actions to avoid future losses. To do so requires that reports are to be generated, shared, read, and acted upon. Companies are encouraged to consider whether their report should be disseminated to a wider audience.

5.3   It may take years for safety trends to be discerned, and so reporting must be archived and revisited on a timely basis. Near-miss reports should be considered along with actual casualty or incident reports to determine trends. There should be consistency in the identification and nomenclature of causal factors across near-miss and casualty/incident reports.

Related IMO Publishing titles

The following publications might be of interest to you. They may be purchased from authorized distributors. Please visit our website (www.imo.org) for further details.

SOLAS

(Consolidated edition, 2009)

Of all the international conventions dealing with maritime safety, the most important is the International Convention for the Safety of Life at Sea, 1974, as amended, better known as SOLAS, which covers a wide range of measures designed to improve the safety of shipping. In order to provide an easy reference to all SOLAS requirements applicable from 1 July 2009, this edition presents a consolidated text of the SOLAS Convention, its Protocols of 1978 and 1988 and all amendments in effect from that date.

Arabic	IE110A	ISBN	978-92-801-5218-0
Chinese	IE110C		978-92-801-6074-1
English	IE110E		978-92-801-1505-5
French	IE110F		978-92-801-2425-5
Russian	IE110R		978-92-801-4268-6
Spanish	IE110S		978-92-801-0198-0

SOLAS on CD (V7.0)

(2009 edition)

This CD provides a consolidated text of the SOLAS Convention, its Protocols of 1978 and 1988 and amendments in force as on 1 July 2009. A comprehensive cross-referencing and indexing system allows the user to navigate easily between the provisions of the Convention, its annex and related texts. Pages of the text and of the on-screen manual can be printed out.

English	DG110E	ISBN	978-92-801-7029-0

SOLAS on the Web

This is a yearly subscription to the SOLAS Convention. It is regularly updated and contains existing SOLAS amendments and amendments not yet in force.

It provides users with access to:

- Logical and easy-to-understand indexes
- Cross referencing with hundreds of internal links
- Clear tables for easy reference

English   S110E

Visit www.imo.org for your local distributor

4 Albert Embankment • London SE1 7SR • United Kingdom
Tel: +44 (0)20 7735 7611 • Fax: +44 (0)20 7587 3241
Email: sales@imo.org
www.imo.org

IMO
INTERNATIONAL MARITIME ORGANIZATION

PUBLISHING